Future Tech

From Personal Robots to Motorized Monocycles

Future Tech

From Personal Robots to Motorized Monocycles

By Charles Piddock

Dr. James Lee, Consultant

NATIONAL
GEOGRAPHIC
Washington, D.C.

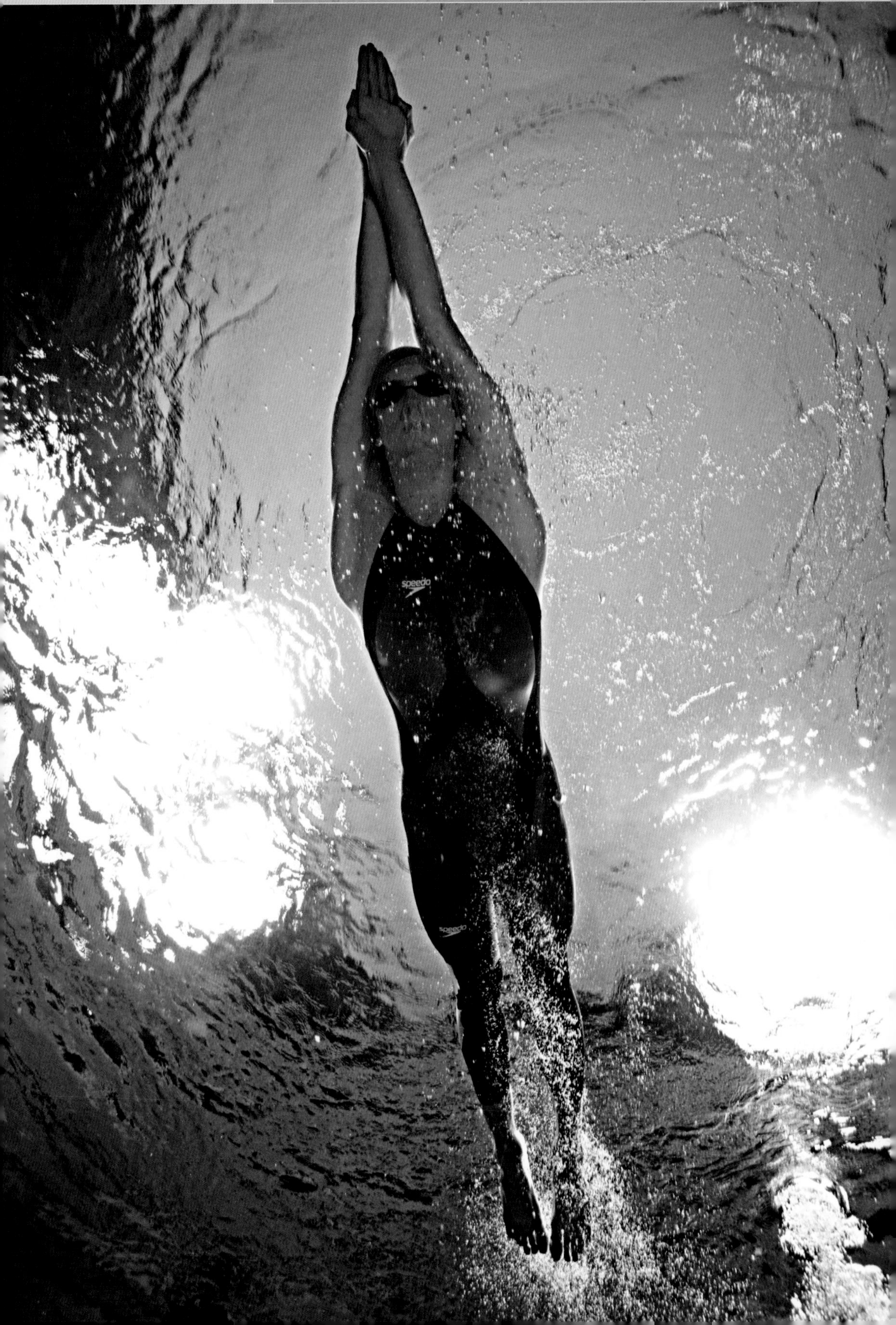
speedo
speedo

Contents

◁ Olympic champion Michael Phelps wore a hydrodynamically advanced swimsuit in the 2004 and 2008 games. The suit's designers were inspired, among other things, by sharkskin, which has tiny scales that streamline the shark's body and enable it to swim faster.

< Automakers hope to bring the electric car to market by 2010. Some will be able to travel 40 miles (64 km) on battery power alone, after which a small gasoline-powered generator will power the battery.

About a half century ago, I was intrigued by the movie *The Time Machine,* a visual adaptation of the novel by H. G. Wells. The book is classical science fiction and portrays the story of a scientist who invented a machine which enables one to travel back and forth in time, so the time traveler can find out what the future will be. Trained rigorously as an engineering scientist, I am interested in futurology. Unlike science fiction, futurology is a discipline of predicting

∧ Dr. James Lee

probable future events based on scientific, systematic, and pattern-based studies of the past and the present. What is the excitement about the likelihood of future events, especially in the technological arena? Here I just mention two fields. Nanotechnology refers to the study of matters on the scale of the nanometer, i.e., one billionth of a meter, and hence it involves understanding, developing, and eventually controlling materials at the atomic scale. Biotechnology links biology (including genetics, molecular biology, biochemistry, cell biology and embryology) and various engineering disciplines for multiple applications, especially for the diagnosis and treatment of diseases. Think of an amputee who regains function via a bionic limb that can be controlled by thoughts through a brain-computer interface. A cure for cancer may lie in the ability to deliver drugs directly into the cancer cells, thereby killing all the malignant cells without harmful side effects. These are not dreams featured in science fiction novels. Many scientists and engineers have been working on these technological frontiers; amazing progress has been made almost every day; and these scenarios will become reality in the not-too-distant future. My young friends, if you become interested in some of the technical areas mentioned in this book, I would urge you to be a participant and make contributions to a probable and preferable future.

James Lee

∧ Jay Schiller uses a bionic hand developed at Rutgers University to play an electronic keyboard. Electrodes pick up signals from Schiller's nerves and direct the motors in the limb.

V 1940 · Elsie the tortoise robot was developed to study simple reflex actions. Unlike robots that came before, Elsie reacted to her environment.

Λ 1946 · J. Presper Eckert, (foreground left) and John W. Mauchly (leaning against pole) are pictured with the Electronic Numerical Integrator and Computer (ENIAC). The first electronic digital computer was developed to help with weapons research during World War II.

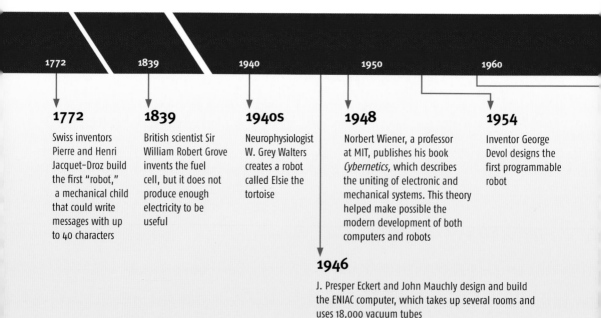

| 1772 | 1839 | 1940 | 1950 | 1960 |

1772

Swiss inventors Pierre and Henri Jacquet-Droz build the first "robot," a mechanical child that could write messages with up to 40 characters

1839

British scientist Sir William Robert Grove invents the fuel cell, but it does not produce enough electricity to be useful

1940s

Neurophysiologist W. Grey Walters creates a robot called Elsie the tortoise

1948

Norbert Wiener, a professor at MIT, publishes his book *Cybernetics*, which describes the uniting of electronic and mechanical systems. This theory helped make possible the modern development of both computers and robots

1954

Inventor George Devol designs the first programmable robot

1946

J. Presper Eckert and John Mauchly design and build the ENIAC computer, which takes up several rooms and uses 18,000 vacuum tubes

> 2008 · Dr. Ben Whalley (left) holds Gordon the robot and Professor Kevin Warwick (right) holds Gordon's biological brain.

∨ 1976 · A model of the Viking 1 Lander that NASA sent to Mars in June 1976

> 2007 · Domo the robot has been designed to hold objects and aid people with simple tasks.

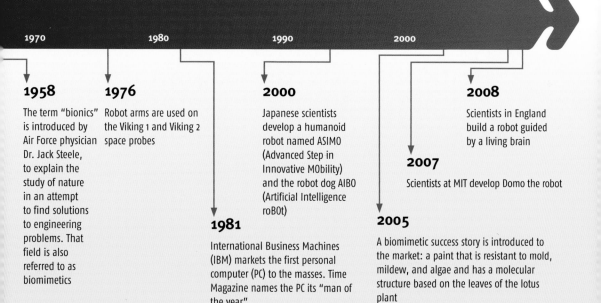

1970   1980   1990   2000

1958

The term "bionics" is introduced by Air Force physician Dr. Jack Steele, to explain the study of nature in an attempt to find solutions to engineering problems. That field is also referred to as biomimetics

1976

Robot arms are used on the Viking 1 and Viking 2 space probes

1981

International Business Machines (IBM) markets the first personal computer (PC) to the masses. Time Magazine names the PC its "man of the year"

2000

Japanese scientists develop a humanoid robot named ASIMO (Advanced Step in Innovative MObility) and the robot dog AIBO (Artificial Intelligence roBOt)

2005

A biomimetic success story is introduced to the market: a paint that is resistant to mold, mildew, and algae and has a molecular structure based on the leaves of the lotus plant

2007

Scientists at MIT develop Domo the robot

2008

Scientists in England build a robot guided by a living brain

11

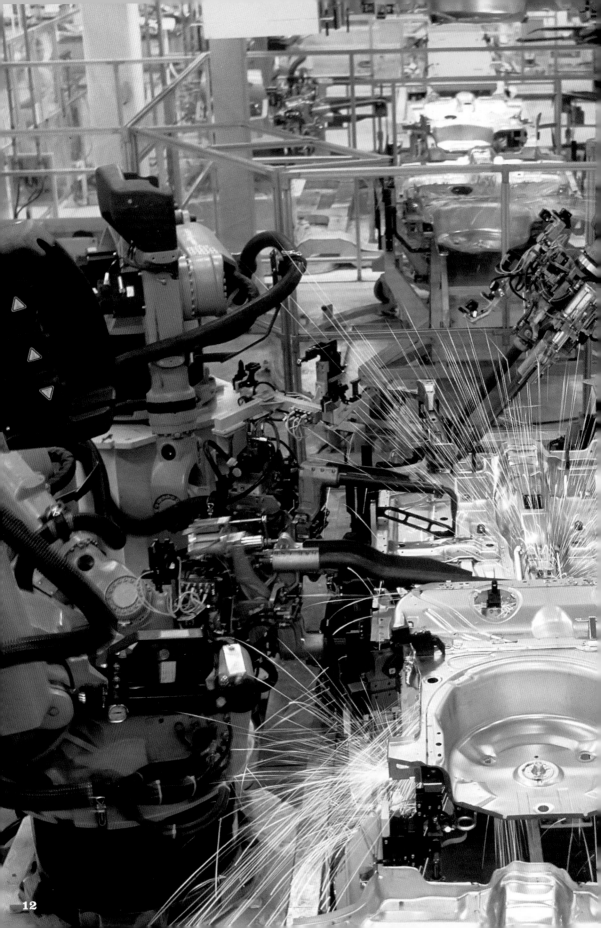

Robots With a Human Face

Making a More Perfect Machine

Dr. Cynthia Breazeal and her team of scientists at the Massachusetts Institute of Technology (MIT) are faced with a major challenge. They are roboticists—scientists who study robots—and their challenge is to build a truly intelligent, friendly robot.

The world is already filled with robots, most of which do not look the least like mechanical humans. On automobile assembly lines, robot arms tirelessly whirl and bend, welding car parts with perfect precision. Police forces use small mobile robots that look like little armored vehicles to defuse bombs

< A robot works on an assembly line in a vehicle manufacturing plant.

13

and investigate places where it is too dangerous for humans to venture. In hospitals, robotic arms perform delicate surgeries. In war zones, flying, pilotless robots with electronic sensing devices report on enemy movements and launch deadly missiles.

Still, as Dr. Breazeal knows, something is missing. Today's working robots, even the best ones, are limited. Their brain power cannot begin to match that of humans, dogs, or even ants.

To robot fans, this is very disappointing. Why can't we build "real" robots like C3PO and R2D2 from *Star Wars,* Lieutenant Commander Data from *Star Trek: The Next Generation,* or even Rosie the robot maid from the 1960s cartoon series *The Jetsons?*

Kismet, Domo, and Leo

He may not have been C3PO, but the most famous robot built by Breazeal's team was Kismet, a robot head that is now retired. Kismet was a sociable robot that has the ability to express itself through humanlike facial expressions. Kismet could frown, look puzzled, smile, and even look sad. It was equipped with visual and auditory sense inputs (eyes and ears) linked to powerful computers outside Kismet's head. When Kismet heard a human voice, it could turn its eyes toward the sound. Tiny cameras behind its eyes and electronic devices in its ears could pick up signals and send them to the computers. The computers then analyzed the signals and told Kismet what facial reactions to express and

∨ The Da Vinci surgical system is actually a network of robots that assists doctors and researchers with work requiring a precise and steady hand.

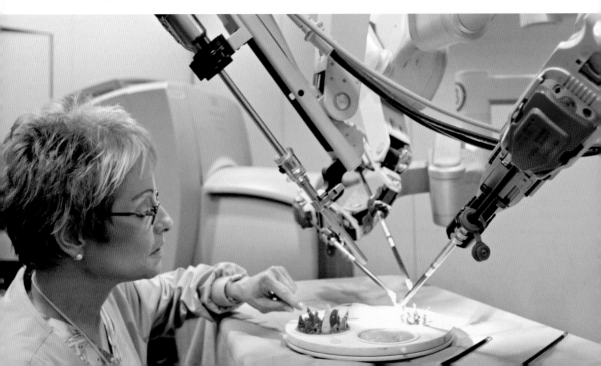

what to say. The robot could speak using a voice synthesizer and sounded much like a little child. Each of Kismet's eyebrows could lower and furrow to show frustration, move upward to show surprise, and slant to show sadness. Visitors who have seen Kismet in action report that it was strange how much the robot seemed like a human being.

Mobile robots are the next generation to emerge from high-tech robotics labs. Two examples are Leonardo (Leo for short), also developed by Breazeal and her team, and Domo, built under the direction of roboticist Rod Brooks, the head of the MIT Artificial Intelligence Lab. Leo is a three-foot-tall robot with big eyes, large pointed ears, a mouth with soft lips and tiny teeth, a furry belly, and furry legs. Domo has no fur. He is all metal, has a long neck, and displays very large blue eyes. Robots like Leo and Domo are wirelessly linked up to a series of 12 powerful computers. The computers are the robots' brains. Both are able to recognize faces, express understanding, and, unlike Kismet, volunteer to help humans do simple tasks. While they are not as expressive as Kismet, they have advanced abilities to learn on their own.

According to Aaron Edsinger, Domo's designer, the robot is the "next generation" of sociable robots after Kismet. "The real potential of robots in the future is going to be realized when they can do many

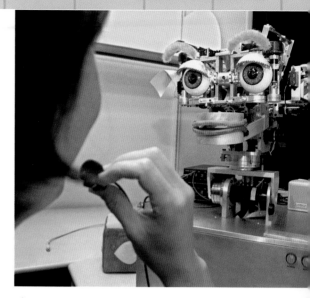

∧ The robot, Kismet, built by Dr. Cynthia Breazeal, is designed to interact with people.

types of manual tasks, including those that require interaction with humans."

Wakamaru

In Japan, a robot named Wakamaru, built by Mitsubishi, may be the world's most sociable self-contained robot. Wakamaru is designed to help and serve people in a friendly, caring, intelligent manner. It knows 10,000 Japanese words and can converse with people. Wakamaru does not have the facial expressions of Kismet, but it can recognize faces and talk with individual people on appropriate topics, such as the weather or sports. For instance, if you told Wakamaru previously that you had a cold, the next time it rolls up to you, it will recognize your face and ask if you still have a cold.

Wakamaru uses body gestures in the same way that humans do. It

Robot Tales

"Kill all humans! Kill all humans!"

In an episode of the animated TV show *Futurama*, which takes place in the year 3000, Bender the robot starts repeatedly shouting those words in his sleep. Of course, it makes Bender's human pal, Fry, just a little bit nervous.

Bender's unconscious desire makes viewers laugh, but in many legends, stories, books, and movies, robots have been anything but characters to laugh at. They have more often been portrayed as machines that spiral out of control, bent on destroying their creators and the human race.

In the early 1900s, when movies were becoming popular, monster robots were everywhere. In one early movie, *The Doll's Revenge* (1907), animated dolls attack furniture and humans. In *The Mysterious Dr. Satan* (1940), an army of evil robots tries to conquer the world. In the 1938 radio drama *War of the Worlds,* giant robots from Mars land in New Jersey and destroy everything in their path with flame-throwing weapons. Eventually robots were also portrayed in a positive light. In *Lost in Space,* a TV series of the 1960s that was made into a movie in 1998, a robot, B-9, called out "Warning, warning" whenever danger threatened humans. B-9 became a kind of celebrity robot. Friendly robots became even more common in the 1970s and 1980s with the arrival of C3PO and R2-D2 of *Star Wars* fame. The 1999 film, *Bicentennial Man* starring Robin Williams told the story of a robot that developed emotions.

waves its arms when it speaks and adjusts the volume of its voice automatically to suit the topic it is talking about. It knows its owners' daily and weekly schedule of waking up, eating, working, and sleeping. At night, it will ceaselessly and noiselessly patrol the house, alerting its sleeping owners to any unusual activity. In the morning, it can wheel into the bedrooms and wake its owners up with a gentle reminder. Wakamaru is also capable of sending email and text messages.

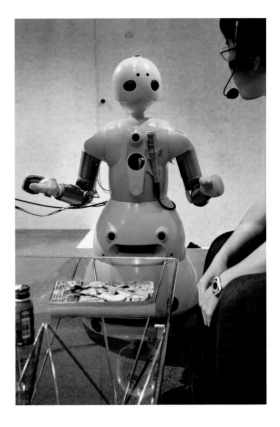

> **Wakamaru is a rechargeable robot that specializes in communication. It responds to verbal requests and uses the Internet to gather information for its owner.**

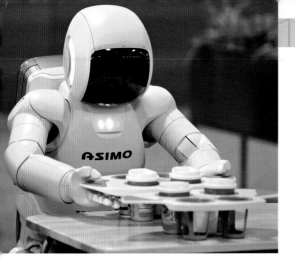

< ASIMO, developed by the Honda Corporation, is capable of performing various actions, including greeting people, serving drinks, walking hand-in-hand with someone, and simulating exercise movements.

Robot Caretakers

Mitsubishi designed Wakamaru to be a friendly robot companion for elderly and disabled people. Japan has a rapidly increasing elderly population and not enough younger people to take care of them. The Japanese hope that Wakamaru and other people-friendly robots will fill this caretaker role. Honda, another Japanese company, has also built a personal robot, called ASIMO (Advanced Step in Innovative Mobility). Instead of rolling on wheels, however, ASIMO walks on two stumpy legs.

Japanese consumers also can buy small personal assistant robots named R100. The R100s, which resemble cartoon characters, can turn on a TV or air conditioner and respond when spoken to.

Japan also has helpful robots in department stores and even hospitals. In one Japanese hospital north of Tokyo, a child-size white-and-blue robot wheels about in waiting rooms and corridors, guiding patients to and from the surgery area. The robot prints out maps of the hospital and even checks blood pressure if requested.

If robots can be made increasingly intelligent and sociable, scientists are well on their way to creating a real-life Rosie and, perhaps, eventually, a humanoid robot such as Lieutenant Commander Data.

Robo-Surgeons

Robots are beginning to revolutionize medicine, especially surgery. A growing number of hospitals across the country now use robotic surgical systems. Such systems enable surgeons to perform even the most complex and delicate procedures through very small incisions. After making tiny incisions in the patient's body, supersteady and precise robotic arms, guided by a human surgeon, make tiny, delicate movements to cut out a cancerous tumor, for example, without touching a complex web of nerves. Throughout the operation, the surgeon controls every movement of the robotic arms, which, much like human arms, can rotate and move in any direction. This allows the surgeon to maneuver precise instruments exactly as needed, even within a very small space inside the patient's body. Robot operations cause significantly less pain and less loss of blood than conventional surgery. Recovery time is much shorter, even for major operations, and patients can return to their normal daily routines much more quickly.

Meet a Roboticist

Aaron Edsinger is a researcher at the Massachusetts Institute of Technology Computer Science and Artificial Intelligence Laboratory. He is the designer of the robot, Domo. Edsinger's mission is to build robots that will help people.

When and why did you decide to pursue a scientific career designing robots?

I came to robotics through being an artist. Initially I was interested in building robotic sculptures [to explore] what it means for something to be alive and to have a personality. This interest led me to MIT for graduate school in 2000. At MIT I discovered that I really enjoyed the scientific research side of building robots. Eventually my interest in the science of robots overtook my artistic passion.

What do you find is the most rewarding part of your job?

The best part is seeing our robot creations 'come to life.' After spending months of thinking, designing, and problem-solving, it is always a thrill to see the machine move and behave in interesting ways. The humanoid robot Domo has numerous different software and hardware components. Even though I developed these myself, at some point I lost track of what each one is doing and how it is interacting with the robot. At this point, Domo sometimes seemed 'alive,' because it wasn't always easy to explain why it did something. One time it reached out and grabbed my hand when I wasn't paying attention. It was eerie and thrilling.

As a child, were you interested in becoming a scientist? If not, what did you want to become?

My childhood hero was Thomas Edison. I read a lot of fiction and nonfiction books on inventors. I always wanted to have my own inventor's laboratory. I wired up our house with a homemade telegraph, built a hovercraft out of my Mom's vacuum cleaner, and built a go-cart out of my Dad's lawnmower.

You've built a robot named Domo. Does it have a sense of humor?

Domo definitely doesn't have the intelligence to have a sense of humor, although it has certainly made me laugh. One time I was wrestling with it, trying to get it to grab a ball. A bug in its code made Domo give me a gentle [punch] to the chin, as if it didn't like what I was doing to it. Of course, Domo didn't know it had done it, but it was funny. Humor is such a ...complicated expression, I think it will be a long time before robots can truly understand and express humor.

What are you working on now?

Right now I have a robotics [company] called Meka Robotics. We are making all types of robot body parts: hands, heads, and arms. Robots are at a stage similar to the early days of the personal computer. Currently they are expensive, complicated, and difficult to use. In 20 years I expect they will be as [common] as the laptop and cell phone.

What will the next generation of robots look and act like?

I think robots will become more functional, and more like appliances in the future. These will be simple-minded creatures dedicated to just one or two tasks, like picking up clothes on a bedroom floor. Entertainment robots, perhaps at the mall or at concerts, will [change] the Hollywood vision of our robot future.

What is the most challenging part of designing and building a robot?

Building robots takes a lot of time and patience. A humanoid can take a couple of years to complete, and it is so complex it can be difficult to get all the different systems working perfectly at once.

How would you rate the importance of the research you are doing for the future of humankind?

If you step far enough back you can imagine the immense potential that robots have. They can transform the way we do physical work, care for our elderly, produce food, and how people relate to each other. Imagine that you could 'embody' a remote robot using an interface on your cell-phone over the internet. You could visit a friend or a grandparent across the country.

What would you tell a young person interested in becoming a research scientist or engineer? What does it take?

Find the thing that you are passionate about. It takes a lot of hard work to become a roboticist, engineer, or researcher. Passion will see you through the tough days and will be the biggest reward on the good days.

What has been your greatest disappointment as a robot scientist?

Progress has been much slower than I'd like. Building a robot with just a fraction of the abilities of a person is an extremely challenging problem. We've been making progress, but we still have a long ways to go.

What has been your greatest reward in your work?

It is very rewarding to think that what we are working on will have a positive impact on the world. Someday, when the robot 'revolution' happens, I hope to be able to point to it and say, 'I contributed to that'.

Do you have a robot living in your home with you?

No, but I do have a dog, which will probably be funnier, more entertaining, and more intelligent than a robot for quite some time.

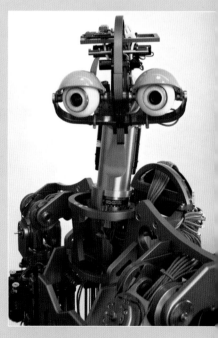

∧ Domo's blue eyes are able to capture everything happening in front of it through the use of cameras, which send information to computers that analyze the input.

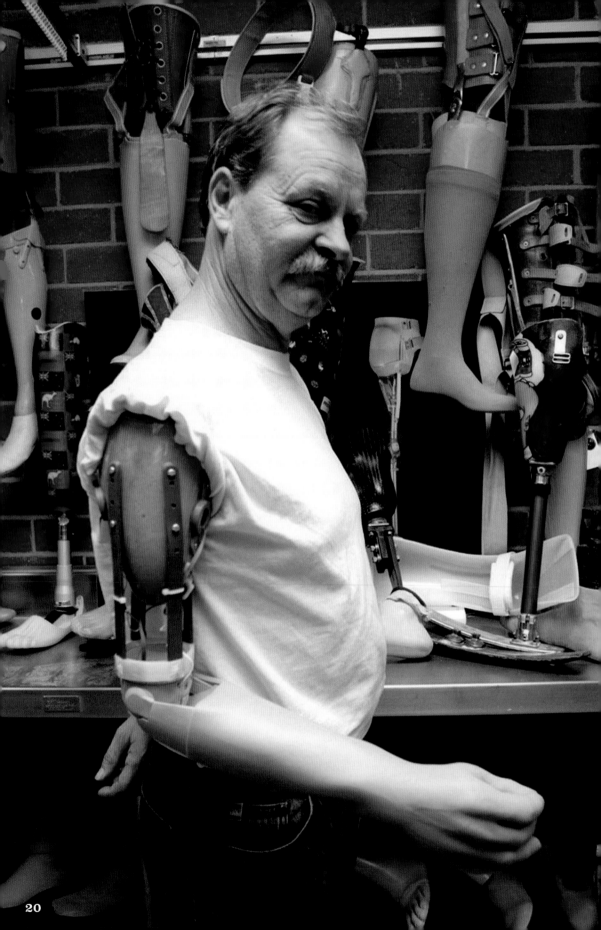

Cyborg Dreams

CHAPTER 2

Building the Bionic Human

Cyborgs, beings that are part natural and part artificial, have long been part of science fiction stories and films. Technology, however, has caught up with myth and the fact is, real cyborgs walk among us. Scientists are creating cyborgs by attaching artificial limbs developed in laboratories to human beings who have lost body parts. These limbs are bionic. Bionic limbs and organs use electronic devices to move.

Comic book superhero fans know who Cyborg is—one of DC Comics' Teen Titans, part human and part machine. After being horribly mutilated,

< In 2005, Peter Eberle, a train driver who lost his arm in an accident, became the first person to be fitted with a new bionic arm that responds by changing muscle movements into electronic impulses.

teen Victor Stone is outfitted by his scientist father with experimental prosthetics (artificial body parts). Victor becomes a cyborg—half human, half machine—a creature with superhuman strength and superior intelligence.

Of course, the story of Victor Stone is only science fiction. The recent advances in robotics, electronics, and miniaturization that have made the age of cyborgs a reality don't include giving people the strength or powers of fictional superheroes. But bionics has made a number of breakthroughs.

A Bionic Hand

In Britain, scientists have created the world's most advanced bionic hand, the i-LIMB.

"The hand has two unique features," explained Stuart Mead, head of Touch Bionics, developers of the i-LIMB. "The first is that we put a motor in each finger, which means that each finger [can be operated independently of the other fingers]... The second is that the thumb is rotatable through 90 degrees, in the same way [human] thumbs are."

The hand works using two electrodes on the skin. Electrodes are devices that conduct electricity from a battery or other electric source. The electrodes pick up myoelectric signals, which are signals created by the contraction of muscle fibers in the body. Normally you have to contract a muscle to

move a finger or open and close your hand. A person with an i-LIMB hand contracts the muscle in the same way, sending myoelectric signals through the electrodes to a small computer in the back of the hand, which interprets the signals and controls the hand. The result is a hand that behaves just like a biological hand, only slower.

The i-LIMB hand has already been fitted on 200 people, including U.S. soldiers who lost their hands fighting in Iraq. U.S. Army sergeant Juan Arredondo, who lost an arm in Iraq, was thrilled to get the i-LIMB

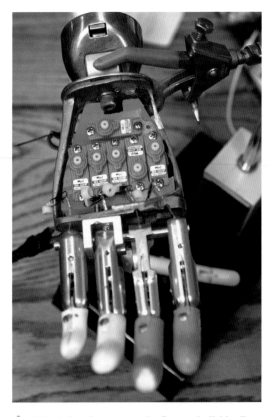

∧ A bionic hand can move its fingers individually so recipients can hold a ball, play a piano, and use a pencil.

⋀ Sergeant Juan Arredondo, an Iraq war veteran, demonstrates his i-Limb hand, which flexes and bends like a normal hand.

hand. "Lying up in the hospital bed I really thought I wouldn't be able to do anything, work, or even provide for my family. But I'm doing it now and it feels great," he said. "Every day that I have the hand, it surprises me."

Bionic Eyes

Hands aren't the only bionic body part. Scientists at the University of Washington have developed a remarkable new contact lens. The flexible, biologically safe lens is imprinted with electronic circuits and lights. Researchers built the microscopic circuits from layers of metal about one-thousandth the thickness of a human hair.

⋁ A magnified view of a contact lens with electronic circuits that researchers hope will help visually impaired people through bionic eye implants.

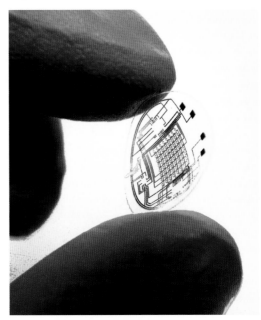

"Looking through a completed lens, you would see what the display is generating superimposed on the world outside," said Babek Parviz, an assistant professor of electrical engineering who helped create the lens.

Like Arnold Schwarzenegger's cyborg character in the *Terminator* movies, the wearer will be able to access a range of visual data. Although much work still has to be done before the new "terminator" lenses are ready for everyday use, scientists can envision a number of uses for them. Drivers or pilots would be able to see a vehicle's speed merely by looking at the windshield. Video-game players could wear the contacts to immerse themselves completely in a virtual world without hampering their range of motion. In the future people will be able to receive traffic information, surf the Internet and access computers—all in the privacy of their own eyelids!

Brain-Computer Interface

Monkeys grabbing and eating marshmallows may not seem like a very exciting event. But at the University of Pittsburgh, the act thrilled a team of scientists led by Dr. Andrew Schwartz, a professor of neurobiology. The team had implanted an electrode into the region of each monkey's brain where voluntary movement originates as electrical impulses. The electrode sent a signal to a mechanical arm

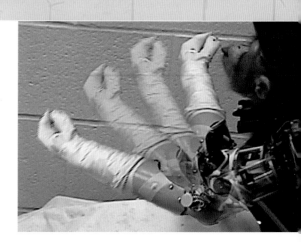

Λ A monkey wearing a robotic arm is able to move it using a brain–computer interface that translates brain signals into actions.

attached to each monkey. In a few days, the monkeys were moving the mechanical arms directly by their thoughts alone, grabbing marshmallow and fruit treats.

Dr. Schwartz's team is beginning preliminary work in humans and plans to implant microelectric arrays, like those used in the monkeys, in human volunteers over the next two years. The scientists hope to perfect a brain–computer interface (BCI) to allow paralyzed people to control not only hands, but all prosthetic body parts and nerve-damaged organs. Electrodes placed on the brain could pick up a brain signal to move an arm or a leg by detouring around a damaged spinal cord.

Cyberkinetics, a U.S. company, has taken BCI a step further with BrainGate, a system that allows paralyzed people to regain some control over their environment. Part of the system is a sensor that is implanted in the area of the brain that controls movement. Another part is a device that picks up signals from the sensor and analyzes the brain signals. In tests, patients have been able to control a cursor on a computer with their brains alone. If people with physical handicaps can use a computer, BrainGate gives them the ability to operate light switches and television, and, eventually, an arm or a leg.

In 2007, Cyberkinetics moved from laboratory research to clinical trials on BrainGate's first patient, Matthew Nagel. Nagel is a stabbing victim who is paralyzed from the neck down. Surgeons attached an array of sensors to Nagel's motor cortex, which is located in the brain just above the right ear. The array is attached by a wire to a plug that sticks out from the top of Nagel's head. The wire is connected to a computer that translates the signal. From his wheelchair, Nagel can open e-mail, change TV channels, turn on lights, play video games, and even move a robotic hand, just by thinking.

∧ Timothy Surgenor, president of Cyberkinetics, poses in front of a model of a brain. The computer screens indicate different types of brain activity.

Going Organic

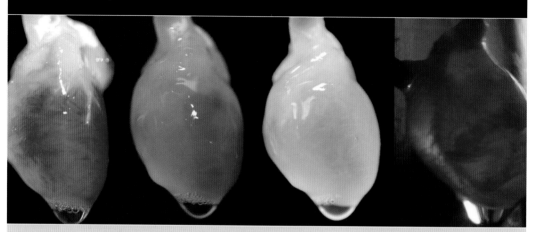

∧ The different stages of creation of a bioartificial rat heart that was developed in a lab by introducing healthy cells into the dead organ. Researchers hope to use this technology to create organs for people in need of transplants.

Most people with lost or damaged body parts would probably prefer real arms, legs, and other body part replacements over ones made of metal and plastic. In the future that may be possible. Scientists are developing ways of growing new tissues and organs from scratch using living cells. In 2008, researchers at Massachusetts General Hospital announced the construction of a bioartificial heart. The team first stripped all the cells from a rat heart, so that only the outline of its muscle structure remained. Then they "seeded" this basic structure with heart cells from a newly born rat. They placed the heart in a culture medium designed to encourage growth. In two weeks, the heart had regenerated and started beating. Other researchers at the University of Missouri are pioneering "organ printing." They lay down cells on a sheet of cell nutrients in the pattern of an organ, similar to the way printers put down words on paper. So far, the team has created a network of functioning blood vessels. The hope behind all these processes is that someday they can be combined with bionics to grow body organs to replace ones damaged or destroyed.

Gordon the Frankenbot

Researchers not only are making systems that could someday connect a living brain with a robotic device, they've also now made a robot with a living brain. Meet Gordon, the Frankenbot. Gordon is the creation of a team of scientists at the University of Reading in England led by Kevin Warwick and Ben Whalley. It is the world's first robot with an organic brain. Gordon's brain is composed of some 50,000 to 100,000 nerve cells that the scientists obtained by taking cells from the brains of unborn rats and growing them in a nutrient-rich culture until they sent electric impulses to each other similar to a normal brain. Because Gordon's brain is organic, it must stay in a special temperature-controlled unit. It communicates with the robot's body through a radio link. To some extent, Gordon learns things by itself. When it rolls into a wall, for example, its sensors send a signal back to its detached brain. The next time, it doesn't make the same mistake—thanks to its living brain.

Warwick and Whalley hope that experiments using Gordon will provide important information about how neurons work in the human brain. "[Gordon provides] a simplified version of what goes on in the human brain where we can look—and control—basic features in the way that we want. In a human brain you can't really do that," said Warwick.

Downloaded Brains

A robot with a living brain is amazing. But even more amazing things involving the brain might be available in the future. "Realistically, by 2050," predicted futurologist Ian Pearson, "we would be able to download [the entire contents of a person's brain] into a machine." Futurologists, also known as futurists, study present trends to predict what is likely to happen in the future. By 2080, Pearson said that just about

everyone will be able to download their brains into a humanoid robot that will prolong their lives indefinitely in cyberspace.

Which Gordon Am I?

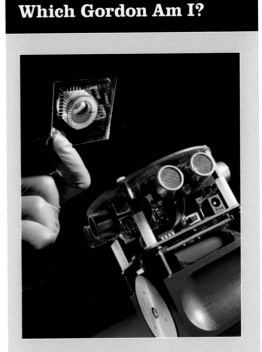

∧ A researcher's hand above Gordon the Frankenbot holds the collection of neurons that pick up electrical activity from the robot's brain and transmit a signal via Bluetooth to control its movement.

Walking into the lab on any given day, researchers may not know what awaits them. Gordon actually has three different brains scientists can link to the robot. Even though Gordon's simple brain is made up of only a small amount of neurons, they are enough to give the robot a personality—actually a split personality. "It's quite funny—you get differences between the brains," said Kevin Warwick, one of Gordon's creators. "One is a bit boisterous and active, while [the other] is not going to do what we want it to."

Nature Tech

Animals and Plants Help Design the Future

When most people think of how scientists and engineers develop new technologies, they imagine high-tech laboratories or chalkboards covered with advanced equations. But some amazing discoveries have come from steamy jungles, bone-dry deserts, windswept mountains, and churning tropical seas. Over hundreds of millions of years, nature has equipped plants and animals with some amazing ways of coping and surviving. These organisms provide useful models for everything from better air conditioners to faster, more fuel-efficient airplanes and cars.

< Many medicines have been developed after scientists applied biomimetics to the study of plants found in rain forests, including those that fight cancer, fungus, and bacterial infection.

The Science of Biomimetics

Applying designs from nature to solve problems in engineering and science is called biomimetics. Throughout the world, biomimetics has emerged as a growing movement to create products for the future.

In order to design energy-efficient buildings, Australian architect Mick Pearce studied termite mounds in the African country of Zimbabwe. He designed ventilation tunnels modeled after those in termite mounds to cool a building, using one-tenth the energy used to air-condition similar buildings. "A termite nest," said Pierce, "is a system like our bodies. It is self-regulating temperature-wise, and that...is an excellent model for a building."

Just about anything in nature can provide the spark for a new invention or technological improvement. In 1982, German botanist Wilhelm Barthlott, who was studying the leaf of the lotus plant, discovered a chemical that, when added to paint, makes it able to repel water and resist stains for years. Biologist Frank Fish of West Chester University in Pennsylvania has helped design new, efficient wind turbine blades based on the structure of whale fins. Mercedes-Benz has designed a new car based on the shape of the blowfish that resembles a cube. Tests show that the design improves the airflow around the car, boosting its gas mileage as high as 70 miles (113 km) a gallon.

◁ The blowfish, with its boxy, cube-shaped body, is streamlined and able to maneuver in tight spaces, something the design team at Mercedes-Benz wanted their cars to be able to do.

Cocklebur Science

Perhaps the most famous example of biomimetics happened by accident. During a hike with his dog in 1948, Swiss engineer and inventor George de Mestral was annoyed by the cockleburs that stuck to his pants and his dog's fur. Examining the burs more closely, he discovered that their spines were tipped with tiny hooks that attached to the loops in the fabric of his pants. De Mestral also noticed how strong the cockleburs were, and he began to think that something this durable and clingy would be useful to humans. He worked with cloth weavers to develop

∧ A cocklebur has thousands of small hooks that attach to the loops of fabric and fur it touches.

a type of fabric that uses tiny hooks and loops to stick to itself. He called it Velcro. The word "Velcro" comes from the French words velours (velvet) and crochet (hook). Velcro is now used all around the world in hundreds of ways, including on shoes in place of laces, on clothing in place of zippers, and anywhere buttons, buckles or adhesives are needed.

One of the hottest areas of biomimetics is medicine. Some of history's great advances in medical research have come from observing nature, then reproducing what nature does. One of the most important has been the development of synthetic insulin. Insulin is a hormone secreted by the pancreas. It is essential for the regulation of blood glucose. People with severe diabetes cannot produce insulin. Insulin was discovered in the 1920s by two Canadians, Frederick Banting and J.J.R. Macleod. Both were given the Nobel Prize in Medicine in 1923 for their discovery. Insulin injections, however, were a problem. Most insulin had to be obtained from cows, pigs, or salmon. The animal insulin worked, but it caused immune reactions in some patients. Scientists continued studying the molecular structure, and in 1978 synthetic insulin was developed.

< A computer image of a car based on the body of the blowfish

Sharkskin Suits

Competitive swimmers at the Beijing Olympics in August 2008 broke more world records than ever before. It was a feat that some people attributed to new Speedo Fastskin suits that reduce drag (resistance caused when a swimmer plows through the water). The new suits are a perfect example of biomimetics. Speedo constructed Fastskins using technology inspired by a microscopic view of the skin of sharks. Sharkskin contains tiny, toothlike scales called dermal denticles that create thousands of tiny grooves. Water "races through the microgrooves without tumbling," thus reducing friction, said shark researcher George Burgess. Speedo's new suits do the same thing.

Snake Venom Medicine

A promising area of biomimetics is the study of snake venom. Tony Woods, a biologist at the University of South Australia in Adelaide, is coleader of a project to investigate whether specific chemicals found in snake venoms can be used to destroy the blood vessels that feed cancer tumors. "A tumor is made of tissue," said Woods. "Like tissue in any part of the body, if you can prevent it from developing a blood supply, or interfere with that supply, then you will have an effect on the growth of that tissue."

Woods and his colleagues have found a compound in snake venom that disrupts special cells that line the inner surface of blood vessels. "It causes the cells to separate from one another, which kills them,"

Woods said. When that happens, he said, it prevents the flow of blood to the tumor, starving it to death. Woods did not reveal which snake venoms the team is studying because they plan to patent the chemical compounds derived from the study.

The advantage of such a drug is that it seems able to distinguish tumor cells from healthy cells and only go after certain types of cells associated with the tumor. Traditional chemotherapy often does not distinguish between the types of cells it affects.

Gecko Science

At Stanford University, roboticist Mark Cutkosky is studying the movements of the gecko, a remarkable lizard. In the fifth century B.C., the Greek philosopher Aristotle marveled at how a gecko "can run up and down a tree in any way, even with head downward." Geckos can scoot across even the slickest of surfaces, such as glass and ceramic, almost as if they had special sticky feet.

In reality, however, gecko feet are not sticky—they are dry and smooth to the touch. So how does the gecko do it? Cutkosky discovered that gecko feet owe their remarkable adhesion to some two billion tiny filaments, or hairs, on their toe pads. Each filament is only a hundred nanometers thick. A nanometer is one-billionth of a meter in length.

The gecko's filaments are so small, in fact, that they interact at the molecular level with a surface. Molecules in the gecko's foot attach to molecules in the surface on which the lizard walks.

The Adventures of Stickybot

After Cutkosky and his team had studied gecko foot biology for two years, they built a robot based on gecko technology. They named the robot Stickybot. To make toe pads for Stickybot, Cutkosky and doctoral student Sangbae Kim, the robot's chief designer, created a new fabric. The fabric is made of specially engineered urethane, a type of plastic, with tiny bristles that end in small points. Though not as flexible or sticky as an actual gecko foot, the toe pads hold the small robot securely on walls and ceilings.

But stickiness, Cutkosky found, is only part of the gecko's amazing ability. In order to move swiftly— geckos can race up a vertical surface at 3.28 feet (1 m) a second—a gecko's feet must unstick themselves instantly. To understand how the lizard does this, Cutkosky sought the aid of biologists Bob Full and Kellar Autumn. With their help, Cutkosky outfitted Stickybot with seven segmented toes that stick and release

∧ A gecko lizard

just like the gecko's toes. He also gave the bot a gecko-like stride that keeps it snug to a wall. Stickybot climbs walls a lot slower than a real gecko, but it easily walks up vertical surfaces made of glass, plastic, and glazed ceramic tile.

Cutkosky sees a huge range of uses for Stickybot's descendants, including climbing sheer cliffs for scientific research and creeping up buildings in police or military assignments, and the entertainment value is limitless. "I'm trying to get robots to go places where they've never gone before," he said.

∨ Stickybot has raised interest among Pentagon officials who see spy service in its future.

33

Thinking Small

CHAPTER 4

Nanotechnology Looks Ahead

For many years, engineers had a common way of looking at things: "Think big"—bigger cars, bigger buildings, bigger ships. Now big is not so big in thinking about the future. The new motto is "Think small"—very, very small. Think nanotechnology.

Strictly defined, nanotechnology is the engineering of working systems on the molecular scale, the art of building things only a few molecules big. A nanometer, after all, is roughly the width of three or four atoms. The average human hair, for example, is about 80,000 nanometers wide. To use

< Scientists working in the field of nanotechnology see exciting advances in the future. This digitally created image illustrates nanorobots fixing blood cells within the body. Such creations will probably be possible within the next decade.

another example, the size of a nanometer compared to a meter is the same as the size of a marble compared to Earth.

Smart Dust

∧ Smart dust particles cling to a drop of liquid. Smart dust sensors can detect light and movement. They may one day be used in the military, for building, and in communications.

At least one scientist, Kris Pister of the University of California at Berkeley, sees a robotic future dominated by what he calls "smart dust"—independent "nanobots" (nanorobots) smaller than gnats. Although it would be equipped with sensors and ways to move about, each nanobot would be relatively simple. But if thousands were combined, they would be capable of doing amazing things, said Pister. Sprinkled on a baby's clothing, for instance, the tiny bots could monitor the child's location, sounding an alarm if the baby climbs out of the crib. The bots could also move around the house at night, eating dirt and generally cleaning up. In effect, smart dust nanobots would turn an entire environment into an almost invisible robot, constantly on alert.

Building From the Bottom Up

Nanotechnology aims to actually control the movement and placement of individual atoms. Traditionally, structures are built from existing materials. For example, if you want to build a house, you cut down a bunch of trees, turn them into lumber, and hammer them together. Nanotechnology takes the approach that nature itself employs to make things. Nature joins atoms together to make molecules. Molecules then join together to form the matter that composes all things—from cells to trees to human beings. Using the most advanced techniques of modern chemistry, nanotechnology aims to create new things by sticking atoms and molecules together in ways not found in nature.

Nanoscience and nanotechnology are in their infancy. Nevertheless, nanoengineers have developed a number of projects on the tiniest of scales. Researchers at Cornell University, for example, have developed nanosponges just 20 nanometers across that will absorb pollution if dropped by the billions on an oil spill. At Rice University in Texas, scientists have created nanocars, compound molecules that can move backward and forward using a nanomotor that is powered by ultraviolet light visible only through a superpowerful microscope. Each nanocar is made of 169 atoms and is 3 nanometers wide and 4 nanometers long.

∧ A digital model of the shape of a nanocar illustrates the round "wheels" that enable it to move around the surface of minute objects.

> This is how nanocars appear when viewed through a microscope.

19 nm

"The idea of making a molecule that can roll like a car on a surface is exciting," said Ray Baughman, who directs the NanoTech Institute at the University of Texas at Dallas. Baughman and James Tour, whose team at Rice University developed the nanocars, believe that nanotechnology is the wave of the future. Its applications seem limitless. Baughman and others believe that nanocars can be useful as tools in helping to create chemical reactions necessary to build microprocessors for computers. A microprocessor is the central "chip" that runs a computer. Engineers would be able to work with individual molecules to build tiny processors and memories, eventually building a supercomputer the size of a cell phone.

Nanocoatings on plain glass could produce superefficient solar panels that convert sunlight into electricity for everyone at almost no cost. The U.S. Navy now uses nanotech coatings on nuclear submarines. The coatings keep sea creatures off the hull and almost eliminate corrosion. One company, Nano-Tex, makes fabrics with nanoengineered molecular structures that repel stains and eliminate wrinkles. In the future, say engineers, nanotech clothes will be able to tell the temperature and automatically warm you up or cool you down.

Olgica Bakajin and Aleksandr Noy lead a research team at the Lawrence Livermore National

The Singularity

Ray Kurzweil, an award-winning inventor and futurist, thinks that nanotechnology, combined with rapid advances in computer technology and robotics, will change human life beyond recognition by the time you are an adult. He says that by the 2020s, nanotechnology will allow scientists to create almost any product people want from inexpensive materials. He believes that nanobots will be able not only to stop the process of aging, but also to reverse it, allowing humans to live forever if they choose to. His most dramatic claim, however, is the creation of what he calls "the singularity"—the seamless merger of machine intelligence and human intelligence. Nanobots in the capillaries of the brain would interact with biological neurons, turning everybody into a supergenius, automatically linking up with the world Internet, and allowing people to communicate with other people through thought alone.

Laboratory in California that studies the use of nanotubes, tubes made of carbon that are 50,000 times smaller than a human hair. Bakajin and Noy have found a way to make a membrane out of billions of the tubes. Water molecules can pass through the tiny tubes, but molecules of solids cannot.

A nanotube membrane would be a big help in desalination, removing salt and other solids from seawater so it can be used for drinking water. Current methods are expensive and use a lot of energy. If the nanotube membrane can be perfected, it will help the billion people around the world who do not have access to clean drinking water.

Medical Revolution

One area of life in the future that nanotechnology will most affect is medical treatment. Engineers are

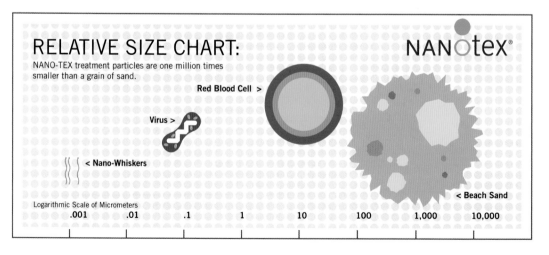

RELATIVE SIZE CHART:

NANO-TEX treatment particles are one million times smaller than a grain of sand.

NANOtex®

Red Blood Cell >

Virus >

< Nano-Whiskers

< Beach Sand

Logarithmic Scale of Micrometers

.001   .01   .1   1   10   100   1,000   10,000

∧ Nanotechnology has created fibers that cause spilled liquids to bead and roll off. The fibers, as seen in this chart, are one million times smaller than a grain of sand.

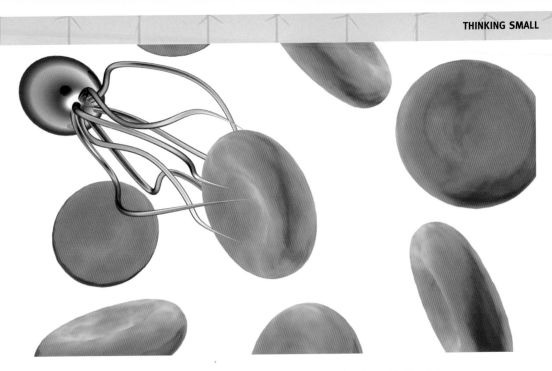

∧ **This artist's rendering shows how a nanobot might travel through a human's bloodstream.**

already on the verge of developing "nanodrugs," tiny particles that can be injected directly into the bloodstream and sent to a specific area of the body. A "targeting molecule," for instance, created in a laboratory using nanotechnology, could find an individual cancer cell and destroy it, curing the disease. Tiny machines could be built to repair cells and correct DNA damage that leads to genetic diseases. Nanocomputers invisible to the eye could be programmed to direct nanomachines that could examine, take apart, and rebuild damaged molecular structures. Bodies could be repaired by nanomachines that mend cells one at a time, fixing a damaged heart or lung, restoring health painlessly and invisibly. Armies of tiny programmed machines could patrol a person's circulatory system, eating cholesterol and repairing weak blood vessels, thus preventing heart attacks and strokes.

Nanotech has already been effective in fighting cancer. Georgia Tech chemistry professor Mostafa El-Sayed was given the 2007 Medal of Science, the nation's highest honor in science for his research on building nanomaterials. Working with his son Ivan of the University of California–San Francisco, El-Sayed is now working to develop tiny gold nano-rods that can bind to cancer cells. Once the rods bind to the cells, they scatter light, which makes them easy to detect. That allows doctors to use a laser to selectively kill the cancer cells without harming healthy cells, which prevents the cancer from spreading.

Electric Vehicle

Motoring Around

CHAPTER 5

A Substitute for the Gasoline-Powered Engine

Despite designs of elaborate flying machines in movies and midcentury predictions of alternate means of travel, cars are likely to remain the way most people around the globe will travel for the foreseeable future. But the ways cars are powered and how they operate will change. The future of the gasoline-powered engine, for example, looks dim. The ever-rising price of oil, along with the danger of global warming caused by burning gasoline and other fossil fuels, has all but doomed the gas-powered internal combustion engine, which has been in mass production since

< California currently boasts the largest number of alternative fueling stations, but as electric cars and vehicles that run on ethanol and other alternative fuels flood the market, new stations are likely to appear around the country.

very early in the twentieth century. Fortunately, scientists and engineers are busy working on alternate ways to power cars, trucks, and buses. What technologies are being developed to replace the gas-burning internal combustion engine? All of them involve different ways to provide power to electric engines.

Plug-In Electric Cars

Some of the best-selling cars today are hybrids, cars powered by both gasoline and electricity. In a hybrid car, an electric battery is recharged by the gasoline motor. In a plug-in electric car, the battery

∧ This car is one of two types of electric vehicles currently in use by London's New Scotland Yard. The vehicles, which are not used for crime-fighting purposes, can reach a speed of 56 miles (90 km) an hour and travel 53 miles (85 km) before needing to be recharged.

can be recharged by plugging it into a standard household electric socket. The technology to produce plug-in cars has been available

∨ The owner of an early model of an electric vehicle plugs the charging cable into his General Motors EVI electric–powered car in Sacramento, California. In the 1970s, a small number of electric cars were built, but there was not enough public interest to keep them in production.

since the late 1800s, but the engines and batteries have not been powerful enough to charge the car for very long or to allow it to achieve high speeds. Now, however, engineers have created plug-in systems that allow cars to go further on one charge and achieve normal highway speeds.

General Motors is developing the Chevrolet Volt, a plug-in vehicle that it hopes to sell in the next few years. The difference between the Volt and hybrid vehicles is

Jet Packs and Atomic Airplanes

It is always tricky to predict the future. Future "experts" have almost always been wrong, particularly in the area of transportation. Here are some transportation ideas that were once wildly popular, but never got off the ground.

Jet packs

During the 1960s, people were fascinated by the idea of jet packs—packs that they could strap on their backs that would lift them in the air and transport them to their destinations (wearing a helmet, of course). Bell Aerosystems developed a "sky taxi" in 1967 that two people could use with a jet pack between them. Unfortunately, the flight lasted only 21 seconds.

Atomic airplanes

After World War II (1939–1945), almost everyone predicted that people would zoom around in atomic airplanes (airplanes powered by atomic energy). Walt Disney, *Popular Mechanics,* and even *National Geographic* joined the bandwagon promoting atomic airplanes. Of course, atomic airplanes were never built. Scientists weren't able to solve problems like containing the heat of an atomic reactor or controlling the dangers of radiation inside the plane, let alone dealing with the real possibility of an atomic explosion.

∧ The Ford Nucleon was never put into production. The design vehicle can be seen at the Henry Ford Museum in Michigan.

Atomic cars

It was advertised as the atomobile, or atomic car. In 1945, *Popular Mechanics* ran an article about a future car zipping around town powered by controlled nuclear explosions. Such a car, said supporters, could be driven 5 million miles (8 million km) without refueling. Testing on the atomic car was halted, however, when it was discovered that a 3,000-pound (1,362-kg) automobile would need an 80,000-pound (36,320-kg) reactor to move it along the highway. Ford Motor Company unveiled its model of the Ford Nucleon in 1958 with a mini-nuclear reactor in its trunk. Unfortunately, it was impossible to shield passengers effectively from deadly radiation.

∧ **The Chevrolet Volt is shown at the North American Auto Show in Detroit in 2007. The car will go into production beginning in 2010.**

that the Volt relies primarily on electric power, whereas ordinary hybrids rely mainly on gasoline power. The Volt does have a small electric engine, but the engine is not connected to the car's drive train—the parts that cause the wheels to turn. The engine is intended to be switched on just to recharge the battery so that drivers will not be stranded on long trips. General Motors is working on developing lighter and better batteries before offering the Volt or a similar car for sale.

Solar Cars

Solar cars use the power of the sun to create electrical power to run a car engine. The first solar car was built by

Australian Hans Tholstrup in 1982. Tholstrup drove the car almost 2,800 miles (4,500 km) between Sydney and Perth (from one side of Australia to the other) in 20 days—10 days faster than the first gasoline-powered car to cover the same distance.

Since Tholstrup's trip, solar cars have progressively become more efficient and powerful because of engineering improvements. The most important improvement is in the efficiency of photovoltaic cells. These flat panels absorb energy from sunlight, generating heat that is converted by the cells into electrical energy. The conversion is called the photovoltaic effect. The energy is then collected by an onboard battery. The battery, in turn, supplies energy to an electric motor that runs the car.

Today's solar cells and batteries are light enough to power experimental cars that can travel 80 miles (129 km) an hour. The car batteries are lithium batteries, the same kind of batteries used in laptop computers, cell phones, and some digital cameras. Solar cars have zero emissions and do not harm the environment. Scientists have yet to solve the solar car's drawbacks: lack of power on cloudy days, damage to the photovoltaic cells by road debris, and the need for a battery that will provide more power for highway conditions.

> Students at the University of Minnesota designed a solar vehicle to compete in the 2005 North American Solar Challenge, a competition to race solar-powered cars across the country.

V A solar car developed in Manila, Philippines, takes a test drive before competing in the 20th World Solar Challenge in Australia in 2007.

The Promise of Fuel Cells

One of the most promising technologies to power automobiles and other vehicles is the fuel cell. A fuel cell is a device that converts chemicals into electricity. Fuel, usually hydrogen, flows into the cell on one side and oxygen flows into the cell on the other side. The mixture of the two results is an electrochemical reaction that changes chemical energy into electricity. A fuel cell is different from a battery because a fuel cell operates as long as fuel flows into it, while a battery runs off energy it has stored chemically. A fuel cell system that runs on hydrogen can be light and compact. Fuel cells generate electricity power quietly and efficiently, without pollution. Their only by-products are heat and water.

One-Wheeled Wonder

∧ **The Wheelsurf runs for about two hours on one tank of gas.**

Monocycles have been around for a long time, since 1869. But today, this mode of travel is available in a new motorized version. For about $7,000 you can buy a Wheelsurf, a motorized monocycle invented in the Netherlands. Wheelsurf can achieve speeds up to 20 miles per hour. The rider sits inside an inner frame on the wheel that contains the engine and gas tank. To turn left or right, simply shift your body weight. Today, Wheelsurf is not allowed on public roads in most countries.

∧ A dashboard display on a Toyota fuel cell vehicle currently in development illustrates for the driver where the energy powering the car is coming from at any given time.

A single fuel cell produces low voltage, so manufacturers stack fuel cells in a series. The more layers there are, the higher the voltage. One of the challenges facing automakers is to stack enough fuel cells to give an automobile the power that drivers are used to in gasoline-powered cars.

Honda, Chevrolet, and BMW have already built cars powered by hydrogen fuel cells. The Honda FCX, which looks kind of like a large jellybean, can deliver 134 horsepower and reach a speed of 90 miles per hour. Beginning in the summer of 2008, customers in southern California were able to lease the FCX for $600 a month.

The major problem with fuel cell vehicles, of course, is getting the fuel to fill their hydrogen tanks. Since fuel cells need to have a constant supply of fuel, drivers will require a chain of hydrogen "gas" stations if fuel cell vehicles are ever to replace gasoline-powered vehicles. To begin, Honda has built ten such stations in southern California to supply customers who leased its FCX model. Many hundreds more, however, will have to be built if fuel cells are to become the power generators of the future.

< A different type of nozzle from the one commonly used to fuel today's cars will be used for hydrogen-powered vehicles (fuel cell cars) being developed by Ford Motor Company.

Living in the Future

CHAPTER 6

What Life Will Be Like...

BRRIIIING! Your alarm wakes you up with a start! Not a very nice way to begin the day. You still have to take a shower, make breakfast, and let the dog out—all before you leave for school at 7:00 A.M.! Look around your home—as far as we have come, we still have to turn our lights on and off, adjust the temperature of the heat and air conditioning, pick up our rooms, and help our parents with the dishes and other housework. Well, in the future, life is going to get easier. Instead of taking care of our houses, our houses will take care of us. We will all live in very smart houses!

< The cartoon series, The Jetsons, featured a family and their dog living in the future. They lived in space, traveled by spaceship, and had a robot housekeeper.

The Jetsons was a popular animated TV show in the early 1960s about the adventures of a family living in the future (2063). The Jetsons live in an apartment kept in order by Rosie, their household robot. Dinner arrives at the press of a button, and everything is automated. Appliances talk and robot devices do all the work.

Will homes in the real future be like the Jetsons' apartment? Scientists and engineers are already working on the home of tomorrow, and it promises to be even more exciting and futuristic than anything on *The Jetsons*. What would your home life be like in 2063, or 2040 for that matter?

First of all, the robot revolution will have progressed and you will be able to have your own Rosie the Robot maid. Your robot will communicate wirelessly with the house itself, which will be an electronically "smart" house.

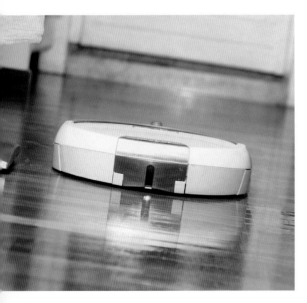

Controlled by a very powerful computer "brain" hidden in the walls, the robot and the house itself will anticipate your every desire. Your household robot will be able to communicate with all the rooms to make sure that things are the way you like them. Your shower will automatically set itself at just the right temperature. Your automated kitchen will know enough to get your favorite breakfast ready at just the right temperature. The latest sports scores will appear on the wall just as you begin to wonder what the scores are. The house will contain not a speck of dust or smudge of dirt because the walls and floors are self-cleaning.

Not a Dream

The possibility of such a dream house in just 25 or 30 years is based on real, down-to-earth scientific progress taking place today. Robots, as you have read, are expected to develop greatly in intelligence and in their ability to work with people. They are expected to play a major role in the combination of what today are called the Internet of things and ambient intelligence.

The Internet of things describes wireless communication not between people, but between things. In the home of the future, for example,

< Household robots are already in use today in the form of vacuum cleaners that roam the premises, silently cleaning.

∧ A smart house tracking system will allow the home's main computer to keep track of who is in the house.

everything will be embedded with radio-frequency identification (RFID) tags. The tags are electronic chips that some stores use today to keep track of inventory. They send out information to an RFID reader. In the future, thanks to developments in nanotechnology, they will be even smaller and vastly more powerful. In the house of the future, for instance, they will tie all kitchen appliances together into a coordinated food preparation system. All the cabinets and the refrigerator will be embedded with RFIDs so that the robot or the in-wall computer will tell you if you are out of ingredients. A screen mounted on the refrigerator will be able to recommend dishes on

the basis of available ingredients sent to the refrigerator by the cabinets. Other computer chips will be able to tell you if a pot of water is boiling on the stove, if the water has been left running somewhere, or if any systems in the home need maintenance.

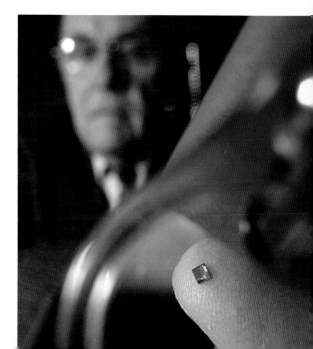

> Radio frequency identification chips like this one work like the bar codes currently in use throughout the world.

Touring the Future in 1939

∧ An exhibit at the 1939 World's Fair in New York showed an elevated highway, now a common sight in many locations.

The 1939 World's Fair was one of the biggest and most popular fairs in history. People from all over the United States and the world flocked to New York's Long Island to see the many exhibits. The theme of the fair was "The World of Tomorrow." One of the most popular exhibits was General Motors' "Futurama." Futurama was a massive scale model, 36,000 square feet (3,348 m²), of what America would look like in 1960. It included futuristic homes, urban centers, and an advanced highway system that permitted speeds of 100 miles (161 km) an hour. New York City in the exhibit had done away with trains, subways, and all public transportation. Instead, seven-lane superhighways were attached to the tops of skyscrapers and actually cut through buildings.

Another highlight of the fair was Elektro and his dog Sparko, robots of the future at the Westinghouse exhibit. Elektro was a giant gold-colored mechanical man. Standing on a platform above the crowds, Elektro stiffly moved around on rollers under its feet. An operator behind the stage with a telephone supplied its voice. The robot moved its head and arms, counted on its fingers, and occasionally smoked a cigarette. Sparko followed Elektro, barking occasionally and standing up on its hind legs. The two wowed the crowds.

Intelligent Walls

Your house will also have what seem like magic walls. The walls will let you customize your environment by changing the walls' color or switching "wallpaper" patterns. Of course, it would not be done by magic, but by the same technology that has already produced superbright, paper-thin TV screens. [Sony has developed a TV screen that is .01 inches (0.3 millimeters) thick.] In the future, this technology, known as OLED (organic light-emitting diode), will be able to make "smart" wallpaper that can change color and patterns or display a large TV or computer screen when you press a button. You will even be able to move the windows in your future home to different places on the wall. OLED walls can be made opaque or clear and can be adjusted by dragging open windows and repositioning them.

The walls and floor will be self-cleaning through advances in nanotechnology. Researchers are working on modifying nanoparticles

▼ An OLED screen is extremely thin and lightweight. The technology will revolutionize displays in the near future.

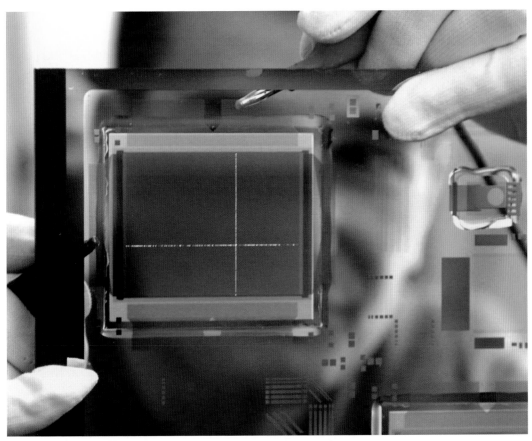

to absorb light at longer wavelengths. This allows the light to kill germs and repel dust.

Ambient Intelligence

Ambient intelligence exists when the Internet of things works perfectly to help people carry out their everyday activities. As devices grow smaller, more connected, and less visible, sensors on our skin, clothing, or in the environment will collect data and "talk" to the other devices that we will rely on in the future. All these devices will be equipped to actually learn from experience. They will be able to observe your habits, likes and dislikes, feelings, and interests, and then feed them into your main computer—the "brain" hidden inside the walls. The computer, like a general commanding an army, will then modify the house to exactly fit what you want. The temperature in the house could be adjusted to suit your average body temperature, for example, so you are always

∧ This remote unit is able to control all aspects of a smart home's functions including temperature, security, and entertainment.

Λ In the connected home as imagined by Microsoft, a central computer would control all aspects of the house's maintenance.

comfortable. Windows will darken when you are ready to sleep and lighten when you want to wake up.

Bill Gates, the founder of Microsoft Corporation, has already built his own smart house. In his house, lights automatically come on when he comes home. Speakers hidden beneath the wallpaper allow music to follow him from room to room. Portable touch pads control everything from TV sets to temperature and lights, which brighten or dim to fit the occasion or match the light outdoors. Visitors to the Gates house take a survey to judge their preferences and then receive a microchip. The chip sends signals throughout the house. When the visitors enter a particular room, lighting and temperature are automatically adjusted to fit their preferences.

In the future, even if you are not Bill Gates, your house will actually seem alive—and magically smart, almost as if it knows what you are thinking.

OOPS! Famous Bad Predictions

Predicting the future is risky business, even if you are an "expert." Here are some predictions by famous people that turned out to be startlingly wrong.

"What can be more palpably absurd than the prospect held out of locomotives traveling twice as fast as stagecoaches?" —*The Quarterly Review,* March, 1825.

"Louis Pasteur's theory of germs is ridiculous fiction." — Pierre Pachet, Professor of Physiology at Toulouse, 1872.

"It's a great invention but who would want to use it anyway?" — Rutherford B. Hayes, U.S. President, after a demonstration of Alexander Bell's telephone, 1876.

"Everyone acquainted with the subject will recognize it as a conspicuous failure." — Henry Morton, president of the Stevens Institute of Technology, on Edison's light bulb, 1880.

"X-rays will prove to be a hoax." — Lord Kelvin, President of the Royal Society, 1883.

"We don't like their sound, and guitar music is on the way out." — Decca Recording, on rejecting the Beatles, 1962.

"The horse is here to stay but the automobile is only a novelty, a fad." — The

∧ **Few would ever have predicted that people would walk on the moon, much less fly freely in space!**

president of the Michigan Savings Bank, advising Henry Ford's lawyer not to invest in the Ford Motor Company, 1903.

"I think that there is a world market for maybe five computers." — Thomas Watson, chairman of IBM, 1943.

"There is no reason anyone would want a computer in their home." — Ken Olson, chairman of Digital Equipment Corporation, 1977.

"Man will never reach the moon regardless of all future scientific advances." — Dr. Lee De Forest, inventor of the vacuum tube and father of television.

What Lies in Store?

Futurologist Ian Pearson studies technology, human behavior, trends, politics, and business in order to make predictions about the future. Although it is not an exact science, Pearson said that he "studies long-term stuff, so (he) usually gets it right." Pearson admitted that he was "wrong, too, about 15% of the time." The work Pearson and others like him do is not gazing into a crystal ball to see what is going to happen 25, 50, or even 100 years from now. Rather, Pearson said he "makes logical deductions for tomorrow based on things we can already see happening."

Here are 10 predictions from Ian Pearson.

By 2025:

- Most families will own a robot that will do many household tasks. Single older people will welcome the extra companionship.
- It will be possible to record and replay sensations, which will make remembering holiday experiences much more intense, as well as improving games and communications.
- Active contact lenses will provide an overlay on everything people see during the day, giving them dual architecture and dual appearance. People will be able to choose how other people see them in the street. These displays could also replace TV and computer displays in our homes.
- Most cars will be electric and will be driven automatically on most roads, linked electronically to the cars around them so that they can drive very close together and eliminate congestion.
- Huge solar power farms will operate in the Sahara desert, providing much of Europe's power via superconducting power lines. The demand for oil will have decreased dramatically, with domestic, industrial, and

transport energy becoming increasingly electric.
- Artificial intelligence (AI) will be superhuman. Most science and engineering will be done by AI, and humans will not be able to understand how some of the resulting technology works.
- It will be possible to design and build simple life forms from scratch, such as single-celled organisms.
- Some machines will have rights. They may have the right to their own independent lives outside of 'office hours', the right not to feel pain, and the rights to own property and even run businesses.
- Magazines and newspapers will have digital paper sections that can show video clips and will be interactive so that people can buy things directly from advertisements.
- Most people will wear digital jewelry. Among other things, jewelry will automatically introduce you to people you would like to meet as you pass them in the street.

▼ Futurologist Ian Pearson

The Years Ahead

∧ Honda's robot ASIMO conducts the Detroit Symphony Orchestra in 2008. The evening was an event to draw attention to the importance of music education for children.

Will your future be filled with robots, smart buildings, nonpolluting fast cars, nanoengineered wonder products, and medical techniques that will prolong your life and make it happier?

Past predictions of future life that were based on ideas about the wonders of technology and science often proved completely false or wildly optimistic. Will that also be true of today's predictions?

It seems unlikely. Futurology, the study of the future on the basis of today's trends, is now a much more exact science. Almost all the predictions that you have read about in this book are based on real science and real discoveries that have implications for the future. Barring world war, disease, famine, or some other horrible development, the world is actually on the verge of a technological and scientific revolution that will change everyone's life for the better. There is no doubt about it—your life will be better and happier in the future. Just wait.

Glossary

adhesion — the ability to stick firmly to something

ambient intelligence — the ability of communications devices embedded in an electronic web to communicate with one another in a seamless manner

BCI — brain-computer interface

capillaries — extremely narrow, thin-walled blood vessels that connect small arteries with small veins to form a network throughout the body

culture medium — a nutrient substance such as a broth or an agar gel in which scientists grow selected microorganisms, fungi, cells, or tissue in a laboratory

cyberspace — the invisible realm in which electronic information exists or is exchanged

cyborg — a being that is part human, part robot

electrodes — conductors through which electricity enters or leaves a battery or a piece of electrical equipment

filament — a slender strand or fiber of a material

fuel cell — a device that generates electricity by converting the chemical energy of a fuel and an oxidant to electric energy

futurist — someone who makes predictions about the future; also known as a futurologist

humanoid — something that has the appearance or characteristics of a human

hybrid car — a vehicle with an engine that can alternate between running on electricity and running on gasoline

incision — a cut, especially one performed by a surgeon

Internet of things — a network of communication among electronic devices without human interaction

microprocessor — the central processing unit that performs the basic operations in a microcomputer, consisting of an integrated circuit contained on a single chip

miniaturization — the process of making a version of something in a much smaller size or on a greatly reduced scale

myoelectric — relating to or involving the electrical properties of muscle

nanometer — one billionth of a meter

nanotechnology — the art of manipulating materials on a very small scale in order to build microscopic machinery

OLED — organic light-emitting diode

photovoltaic cell — a cell that detects and measures light to produce electricity

photovoltaic effect — the process by which sunlight is converted to electric energy

prosthetics — artificial body parts

RFID — radio-frequency identification

roboticist — a scientist who builds or studies robots

voice synthesizer — a machine that creates an artificial voice

Bibliography

Books

Asimov, Isaac. *I Robot*. New York: Bantam Spectra, 2008.

Bridgman, Roger. *Robot (Eyewitness Guides)*. New York: DK Publishers, 2004.

Dregni, Eric, and Jonathan Dregni. *Follies of Science: 20th Century Visions of Our Fantastic Future*. Denver: Speck Press, 2006.

Gerdes, Louise. *Humanity's Future* (Opposing Viewpoints Series). Farmington Hills, MI: Greenhaven Press, 2006.

Ultimate Robot. New York: DK Publishers, 2004.

Articles

Geary, James, "I Robot," *The Observer,* (England), July 13, 2008, p. 29.

Intini, John, "A Short History of the Near Future," *Maclean's* (Canada), October 8, 2007, p. 58.

Marantz Henig, Robin, "The Real Transformers," *The New York Times Magazine*, July 29, 2007, p. 28.

Mueller, Tom, "Design by Nature," *National Geographic,* April 2008, p. 68.

Von Radowitz, John, "Robot with a Rat's Brain," *Daily Record* (Glasgow, Scotland), August 14, 2008, p. 12.

Wilson, David, "Rise of the Robot," *The Age* (Melbourne, Australia), November 9, 2006, p. 4.

On the Web

Robots.net, Robot News and Robotic Info **http://www.robots.net/**

Machine Science **http://www.machinescience.com/catalog/**

FutureCars.com, Cars of the Future **http://www.futurecars.com/**

Science News for Kids **http://www.sciencenewsforkids.org/**

Howard Hughes Medical Institute: Cool Science for Curious Kids **http://www.hhmi.org/coolscience/**

Further Reading

Bever, Mark. *Robotics (Life in the Future)*. Connecticut: Children's Press, 2002.

Cook, David. *Robot Building for Beginners*. Apress, 2002.

Gifford, Clive. *Robotic Hornet: Learn How Hornets Have Inspired the Design of Robots*. Silver Dolphin Books, 2005.

Jefferis, David. *Micro Machines: Ultra-Small World of Nanotechnology*. Crabtree Publishing Company, 2006.

Maddox, Dianne. *Science on the Edge—Nanotechnology*. Blackbirch Press, 2005.

Index

Boldface indicates illustrations.

About the Author

Charles Piddock is a former editor-in-chief of *Weekly Reader,* publisher of sixteen classroom magazines for schools from pre-K through high school, including *Current Events, Current Science,* and *Teen Newsweek.* In his career with *Weekly Reader,* he has written and edited hundreds of articles for young people on world and national affairs, science, literature, and other topics. Piddock also served as a Peace Corps volunteer in rural West Bengal, India. Piddock has also authored *National Geographic Investigates: Outbreak* for the Society.

About the Consultant

James Lee received his B.S. and M.S. degrees from National Taiwan University and Rice University, respectively. In 1971, he received his Ph.D. degree in mechanical engineering from Princeton University. Dr. Lee has been a researcher in National Institute of Standards and Technology (NIST) and National Aeronautics and Space Administration (NASA). He is currently a Professor at George Washington University. His current research interest is in the field of Nano/Bio Science and Technology.

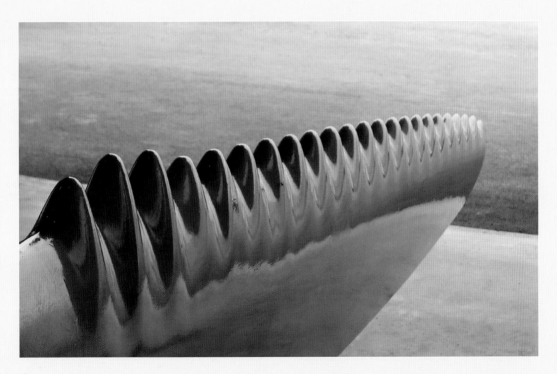

∧ Researchers studied the fins of humpback whales in order to design a more efficient windmill blade.

Founded in 1888, the National Geographic Society is one of the largest nonprofit scientific and educational organizations in the world. It reaches more than 285 million people worldwide each month through its official journal, *National Geographic,* and its four other magazines; the National Geographic Channel; television documentaries; radio programs; films; books; videos and DVDs; maps; and interactive media. National Geographic has funded more than 8,000 scientific research projects and supports an education program combating geographic illiteracy.

For more information, please call 1-800-NGS LINE (647-5463) or write to the following address:

National Geographic Society
1145 17th Street N.W., Washington, D.C.
20036-4688 U.S.A.

Visit us online at
www.nationalgeographic.com/books

For librarians and teachers:
www.ngchildrensbooks.org

More for kids from National Geographic:
kids.nationalgeographic.com

For information about special discounts for bulk purchases, please contact National Geographic Books Special Sales: ngspecsales@ngs.org

For rights or permissions inquiries, please contact National Geographic Books Subsidiary Rights: ngbookrights@ngs.org

Library of Congress Cataloging-in-Publication Data available upon request

Hardcover ISBN: 978-1-4263-0468-2
Library ISBN: 978-1-4263-0469-9

Printed in China

Book design by Dan Banks, Project Design Company

Published by the National Geographic Society

John M. Fahey, Jr., *President and Chief Executive Officer;* Gilbert M. Grosvenor, *Chairman of the Board;* Tim T. Kelly, *President, Global Media Group;* John Q. Griffin, *President, Publishing;* Nina D. Hoffman, *Executive Vice President; President, Book Publishing Group*

Prepared by the Book Division

Nancy Laties Feresten, *Vice President, Editor in Chief, Children's Books;*
Bea Jackson, *Director of Design and Illustrations, Children's Books;*
Amy Shields, *Executive Editor, Series, Children's Books*

Staff for This Book

Virginia Ann Koeth, *Editor*
Jim Hiscott, *Art Director*
Lori Epstein, *Illustrations Editor*
Lewis R. Bassford, *Production Manager*
Grace Hill, *Associate Managing Editor*
Jennifer A. Thornton, *Managing Editor*
R. Gary Colbert, *Production Director*
Susan Borke, *Legal and Business Affairs*

Manufacturing and Quality Management

Christopher A. Liedel, *Chief Financial Officer*
Phillip L. Schlosser, *Vice President*
Chris Brown, *Technical Director*
Nicole Elliott, *Manager*

Photo Credits

Front: Robert Clark/National Geographic Stock
Back & Spine: Mehau Kulyk/Photo Researchers, Inc.
Back Icon: Boston Museum of Science/Visuals Unlimited/Getty Images

AP=Associated Press; 1, Shutterstock; 2-3, Peter Menzel / Photo Researchers, Inc.; 4, Courtesy of Speedo; 6, Shutterstock; 8, Courtesy of Dr. James Lee; 9, 10, AP; 10, Smithsonian Institution; 11, NASA; 11, Image courtesy of Aaron Edsinger; 11, Diem Photography/ University of Reading; 12-13; IStock; 14, 15, 16, 17, AP; 18, 19, Image courtesy of Aaron Edsinger ; 20-21, © Glenn Hunt/epa/Corbis; 22, 23, AP; 23, University of Washington; 24, Image courtesy of Andrew Schwartz; 25, AP; 26, University of Minnesota; 27, Diem Photography/ University of Reading; 28-29 Shutterstock; 30, © 2008 Daimler AG; 31, 33, Photos.com; 33, Mark Cutkosky; 34-35, Shuttestok; 36, Jamie Link, UCSD; 37, Y. Shirai/ Rice University; 38, Courtesy of Nano-Tex, Inc; 39, Shutterstock; 40-41, Visions ofAmerica/Joe Sohm; 42, AP; 43, Ford Motor Company; 44, 45, 46, AP; 46, Courtesy of www.wheelsurf.nl; 47, AP; 48-49, Uckoo's Nest/Hanna-Barbera/Wang Films/The Kobal Collection; 50, IStock; 51, Prof. Olaf Diegel, Auckland University of Technology; 51, 52, AP; 53, Matthias Hiekel/dpa/Landov; 54, Image courtesy of Control4; 55, AP; 56, Photos.com; 57, Image Courtesy of Ian Pearson; 58, AP; 63, Courtesy of Frank Fish

Front cover: A climbing robot with the structure and movement of a gecko.

Back cover: Scanning electron micrograph image of velcro attached to fabric.

Page 1: It is likely that in the future, mobile robots resembling this design will live in our homes and assist us with all sorts of everyday tasks.

Pages 2–3: AIBO (Artificial Intelligence Robot), a robot dog sold as a toy in Japan, barks, falls over, stands up, sleeps, and walks. The robot is controlled by a remote, but also responds to movement.

A Creative Media Applications, Inc. Production

Editor: Susan Madoff
Copy Editor: Laurie Lieb
Design and Production: Luís Leon and Fabia Wargin